Fragments Held By Home

Ketaki Thorat

BookLeaf Publishing

India | USA | UK

Made with ❤ on the BookLeaf Publishing Platform
www.bookleafpub.in
www.bookleafpub.com

Dedication

To the keepers of my heart and memory, thank you for being the home I always return to, in life and in these pages.

Preface

Memory is a curious thing—a suitcase that never quite closes, a collection of moments we carry with us, unpack, and repack as life unfolds. This collection of poetry began as an attempt to reflect on my journey but also as a love letter to those who have shaped it—family and friends who have left an indelible mark on my heart. Their warmth, their kindness, and their enduring presence are the anchors in this ever-shifting world.

These poems are stitched together from the fabric of my life: the laughter of family, the comfort of friendships, the ache of goodbyes, and the endless search for belonging. They are the echoes of meals shared, hands held, and words exchanged across distances and time. Each verse is a snapshot, a thread of memory woven into the tapestry of who I am and who I am becoming.

This collection invites you to look at your own suitcases and attempt to understand the weight of those suitcases; to sit with the joy, the loss, the love, and the longing that accompany us wherever we go. Unpack the memories you hold, and perhaps to find a piece of yourself in these words. May they remind you of the beauty and weight of the stories we carry and the connections that make them worth telling.

Acknowledgements

For the family who raised me and the friends who held me, whose love and presence are the verses that shape my soul and the memories I carry like precious luggage— thank you for filling my life with the kind of love and belonging I'll carry in every word I write.

1. The City That Doesn't Know Your Name

You wake in a city that doesn't know your name.
You ask for directions, and the wind answers
in a language that sounds like words splintering under
the weight of an apology
The air here, heavy with the exhaustion of endless
waiting
You fold into it, try to pass as fog

Someone says, "Smile," and you try-
but your face feels like borrowed fabric, the stitching
coming loose.
Here, even the light is foreign-
burning too quickly through your eyes,
making silhouettes out of everyone you meet.

You run your hands through your hair,
feel the roots straining,
aching for a soil that isn't here.
You map your days by convenience stores,
by streetlights that hum like a trapped throat.

Every corner you turn,
your heart clatters to the floor like loose change.

You think, if you can just find the right street,
if you can just learn how to say "home"
without your voice cracking-
maybe you'll stop feeling like an estranged guest in your
own life.
But still, you walk, feet blistered with possibilities,
the horizon stretching out its arms like a mother who
finally remembers your face.

2. Carry You in My Bones

Do I remind you of someone?
Am I your younger self, mirrored too sharply?
The edges of your past carved into me,
A reflection of all you lost to become
A mother who stayed, a mother who gave.
I stand on the edge of what I've become,
knowing each piece of me was once a piece of you.

The wind is a thief tonight,
stealing the scent of home—
the spices that rose with your laughter,
the hum of your lullaby woven into the walls;
When my meals pile up untouched,
or when the clock spins past midnight and I'm still
awake.
Who will smooth the tension from the back of my neck,
whispering like soft rain, urging me to rest?
Who will tell me to drop the weight in my hands,
to let the world fall away for just a moment?

I chase them in my mind,
but memory is a fragile breeze,
slipping through my hands like grains of salt.
Mother, did I ever thank you

for the dreams you buried
so I could grow?
For the words you swallowed
so mine could bloom?

I carry your silence in my bones,
a quiet hum beneath my skin,
a language I'm still learning to speak.
You taught me how to stitch the world together
with nothing but threadbare hope,
how to hold joy carefully,
the way you held a glass lantern in a storm.

I wonder if I remind you of yourself,
or of the person you might have been
if the world had asked less of you.
But here I am, standing tall on the foundation
of everything you gave away,
built from the quiet sacrifices
you scattered like seeds in a garden,
growing tall with roots deep in your warmth,
bearing the blooms of all you nurtured,
without a single thorn of regret,
only the soft fragrance of love unyielding.

3. Hands That Built My Dreams

Do I remind you to be someone?
A shadow reshaped by the firelight,
moulding myself into something unrecognizable,
smoothing edges, softening flames,
So you could see a reflection worth calling your
daughter.

Yet, I am the foreigner in your house of memory,
half-made of your struggle, half of my own.
I stand in the doorway, always half-leaving,
always half-returning.

There were times I dreamed myself far from you,
a kite straining against the string,
believing freedom was in the letting go.
But now I know the wind that carried me
was the breath of your quiet sacrifice.
Every step I took was over bridges
you built from nothing but resolve,
each stone a story you never told.

Baba, you are the riddle of my becoming.
Even now, I search your hands for answers—

hands that held too tightly, then let go too soon.
How do I thank you for the things you didn't say,
for the lessons stitched in silence,
for the gift of your unspoken faith?
It was never the leaving that hurt,
but the knowing I could always return.

All I dare to dream,
is rooted in the soil of your shadow.
A weight that anchors me to a home
I can carry across oceans, across years.
Now I see—every dream I carry is yours,
its wings shaped by the breath of your prayers.
Every door I open echoes with your steady footsteps,
your lessons whispering like soft rain,
reminding me where I come from, where I belong.

Your hands bore the weight of my dreams,
calloused with labour, yet open with giving.
Each dawn you rose, unbroken by the world,
and each night, you returned with hope enough
to fill the cracks in my ambition.
Today, I stand on the shore of all you've given,
the horizon wide with possibility,
This is the shape of home:
a father and daughter,
each a dream within the other,

each building the bridge
that never burns.

4. Moonlit Cradle of Tides

Our room was a womb,
a shield stitched in secrets,
It's air heavy with the scent of shared years.
Your name was a song I could summon,
always within arm's reach,
stitched into the melody of shared silences,
the weathered sheets holding the weight of our past.
Now I am stranded in a house
that feels hollowed of its own walls,
the echoes of your giggles tucked in the wood,
out of reach like half-forgotten prayers.

My unsent messages grow like weeds,
text blooms in silence,
their roots curling toward the absence in my room—
a grave of memories too tender to bury.
I write, but do not send,
as if words could wake the part of you
still lingering in this hollow space.
I wonder if you would hear me
in the stillness of the moonlight between heartbeats,
where our giggles still linger like a half-forgotten hymn.

Without you, the room shrinks—

its walls press inward,
its shadows grow longer,
its nights stretch into endless alleys of solitude.
You were the moon in my tide,
the slow heartbeat to my restless dreaming.
And now, I am lost in this sea of stillness,
searching for the glowing moonbeam
of your laughter to guide me back.

My sister, find your way to me
or send me a dream where we are whole again,
where our room shelters us both,
and the space is no longer a tomb
but a cradle,
rocking us gently in the arms of what was.

5. Sacred Hollow Light

Your voice, like sunlight tangled in curtains,
brimming with tales you've told a thousand times—
The miles are beasts with iron teeth,
chewing at the edges of my days,
stealing the moments I could have had
watching you laugh,
your face a soft map of joy and age.
Helplessness is an anchor,
dragging me to the deepest trenches of worry,
and still, I cannot reach you.

The thought of losing you—
a shiver I dare not hold too long,
a shadow too dark to name.
What if I am here,
and you are there,
and the world decides it's time to teach me
how to live with the hollow shape of you?
What if your last words
never reach me?
What if your last breath
is lost in the space between us?

But then I remember:

you, bright and alive,
laughing as if the world were nothing but a joke
too sweet to cry over.
You, calling my name
as if it were a sacred chant
only you knew how to sing.
You, with your stories and your faith,
building a home inside my heart
so I can carry you wherever I go.

I pray, not with hands clasped,
but with this poem,
an offering to the wind that travels
where I cannot.
And when that day comes—
when your childlike innocence
joins the stars,
when your unwavering faith
becomes the light
guiding me home—
know this:
I will carry you, always,
Even in your absence, a sacred space
where I find you, again and again.

6. The Garden We Tend

We were sowed in the same soil,
root-bound by a shared womb,
sprouting in the sun of our parents' love.
Your laughter, the first rain I ever heard;
my tears, the first river you ever saw.
We grew side by side,
branches brushing, leaves whispering secrets
only sisters can keep.

But the gardener's hands are never even.
I watered you with patience,
while I soaked in the storms.
You grew wild with thorns to guard my tender parts;
you bloomed steady and soft,
your petals wide enough to shield the both of us.
Still, we were the same flower
in different seasons.

Now I am an ocean away,
Uprooted and replanted
in a land where the frost bites early
and the sun feels borrowed.
The soil here smells foreign,
its language unfamiliar.

I have learned to stretch my roots
toward small patches of warmth,
but I ache for the garden we shared.

You stayed, hands deep in the soil,
tending to what I left behind.
You feed the roots we planted together:
our parents' quiet hopes,
their brittle, ageing stems.
You hold their hands, prune their grief,
water their smiles with your laughter.
You, the new gardener,
doing the work I used to do.
Your care is a song
that makes even the wilting bloom again.

There is no envy between us,
only the soft ache of distance.
I imagine you kneeling in the dirt,
the same dirt that once dusted my palms,
your fingers caked with the history
of who we were.
And I wonder if you can feel my love
trailing through the roots,
a silent whisper carried beneath the ground.

I send my love in messages and calls,

like seeds scattered on a breeze.
You catch them, tuck them into the soil,
and make something grow.
Your voice on the phone
is like rain on parched leaves,
and when you laugh,
I hear the wind moving between us,
braiding us closer than miles would allow.

The garden we grew in is still home,
even if my feet are far from its paths.
You are the keeper now,
tending the roots we planted,
pulling the weeds of worry and fear,
fertilizing the dreams
that once stretched from our lips to the sky.

You are the earth, steadfast and warm,
and I, the restless sky, look down on you.
But even now,
we are the same flower
in different seasons.
We will always bloom together,
a garden that never forgets itself.

7. A Quiet Hand on the Wheel

With quiet force, my father drove me back,
to the place where my shadow fits the walls—
a room that smells of growing,
spilled ink, weathered panes,
and the ghost of a younger me.

He did not speak when my mother's words
swirled like monsoon rain—
It makes no sense. Let it go.
But he, steady as the horizon,
only took the keys,
his silence, a trail I could outline.

The car moved like a heartbeat,
the engine purring low,
its rhythm saying what he would not:
This is love—
a hand on the wheel,
a sacrifice without ceremony.

In his eyes,
the stars of my hometown reflected.
He knew the weight of home—

how it anchors,
how it loosens you.
He knew without my telling,
I needed one last night
to stitch myself into its skin.

When we arrived,
he did not linger.
His hands rested on the wheel
like birds too tired to fly.
He said nothing
as I climbed out,
his silence wrapping me in its comfort.

I slept in that room
like I was burying something,
the sheets pulling over me
like fresh earth.
In the morning, he returned,
his love folded in his shirt,
his face saying:
I will hold this space for you,
even when you cannot return.

When I left again,
it was his hands I thought of—
how they carried my leaving,

how they spoke what his voice never did.
How love
is sometimes nothing more
than driving into the night
and letting your child go.

8. Packed Inheritance

She packed with the care of someone
stitching the seams of their heart.
A scarf folded like an embrace,
a jar of spices humming her kitchen's hymn,
a journal, blank as the sky
on the morning I left.

Carry yourself lightly, her eyes whispered
as if grace were weightless,
as if independence didn't strain the spine.
But her voice—soft, steady—
folded itself into the suitcase too,
tucked between sleeves and shoes,
a whisper to remind me:
You can always come home.

In the stores of a foreign city,
I hear her advice echo in the clang of coins:
Don't let the world convince you
to shrink yourself.
On narrow streets where language falters,
I walk taller, my feet guided
by a strength she lent me long ago.

At night, the scarf wraps more than my shoulders.
It holds her hand on the edge of my dreams,
threading warmth into the places
distance made cold.
She gave me a suitcase,
but what I unpack each day
is her grace—
stitched into my being,
weightless after all.

When I falter in the foreign air,
when loneliness gnaws at my edges,
I picture her hands—steady, deliberate—
tying knots in my fraying courage.
You're stronger than you think,
her voice reminds me,
woven into every hem.

This suitcase, she said,
isn't just for carrying things.
It's for holding who you are,
for bringing pieces of home
to the places you've yet to belong.

9. Maps of Us

We were wide-eyed dreams once,
small towns on the map of our lives,
unclaimed silhouettes, markers of uncharted lands—
The mountains stood like silent gods
over the soft horizon of possibility.
We spoke in laugh-lines,
dreams stitched between our palms.
boundless, where every bend led
to a place we hadn't yet discovered,
our names written on streets we hadn't walked.

But time came,
a map with jagged edges,
unfolding at the seams.
She, a faded line in a forgotten corner,
worn by the weight of cities
that do not remember you.
I, a pin still planted—
in the place where hope gathers like rain,
in the spaces between our dreams,
still calling her name
in the creases of maps we used to hold.

Crossing borders,

her journey curved westward,
her voice a dot on the horizon,
a tiny mark on the line of my life
we couldn't erase.
I stayed,
navigating the streets of memories,
mapping our steps along the lake,
the hill and street food stalls,
the places where we carved our names
in the dust and in each other.

We spoke in coordinates,
our voices stretched between the silence
long-distance whispers
across time zones,
our lives sketched in blue ink,
but never meeting.

Time is a sharp blade,
and it has cut us both in different ways.
She, like a flower pressed dry,
petals still but wilted,
her soul heavy as lead,
heart thumping with the rhythm
of the city streets she can't remember.
I, still a fragment of that girl—
tired, but with light spilling through the cracks,

hope clinging to the space between my ribs,
still believing something might grow
from the dust of all this yearning.

The map shifting underfoot,
my compass pointing north,
to a place where the roads never felt like home.
a land where I had to redraw my map
I searched for home,
but found only shadows,
empty spaces where the warmth of our words
used to live.
The only place that felt like home
was in our old conversations,
in the familiar streets I still walk in my head,
in the lake we watched together,
on the hills where we sat
and let our hearts spill out to the wind.

The roots of our homecoming uprooted
no longer the girls
who ran through its streets with joy,
no longer the daughters of the soil,
but guests.
Like paper dolls—
fading at the edges,
the fabric of belonging unraveling

as we stood in the rooms
where our childhood still whispered,
but never reached our ears.

Time paused where distance shrank at the airport
meeting again where paths cross,
a fleeting intersection
before they split apart once more.
the map of us folding again,
but we were always here,
in the quiet meeting points of our journeys.

I mapped with hesitant hands,
wondering if I could ever draw a line
that led me back to something I called home.
this city of lights,
but not the city of my soul.
The streets hummed,
the museums held their secrets
like closed books I couldn't open.
Not even the space I lived in felt like home—
just walls that didn't know me,
floors that didn't care if I walked on them.
But you—
you were here.
In the crooked alleyways and boulevards,
in the quiet of the café where we shared

our tired dreams and nervous laughter,
in the smell of rain on cobblestones,
in the same light that touched our faces
all those years ago.

Weathered women,
our hearts a little more cracked,
our backs a little more bent,
but we are still here.
Like rivers that meet and part,
our paths will merge,
and then we will scatter,
but the meeting never truly ends.
across continents where our laughter spilled,
the alleys where our footsteps met
like rivers joining,
only to break again.

We are maps of us—
written in places we have been
and places we have yet to go.
Our paths will always meet,
then scatter,
as all maps do.
But no matter how far we travel,
we are the road,

the landmark,
the place we know without looking,
the compass pointing true
back to each other,
across time,
across oceans,
across maps that can never contain us.

10. A Strand of Sugar

You, the festival's first light,
always in the corner of my eyes,
Even in the quietest moments here,
I hear your laughter, loud as temple bells,
filling the empty corners of this foreign place.

Your laugh, it's contagious—
like the first breeze of spring after winter's hold,
lifting the weight from everything,
turning even the hardest moments soft,
light, as if nothing in this world could be wrong
when you are here,
spinning sweetness from air and laughter.
It's like I'm always waiting,
for that next burst of your joy,
and with it, everything feels better.

Some days, I catch the scent of something familiar—
the sweet warmth of waffles, golden and crisp,
or the rich, spiced fragrance of curry,
and for a moment, it feels like you're here—
your presence drifting in the air,
just a breath away, as though time hasn't passed.

How I'd stuff my suitcase with your laughter
and bring it home to sit in every room I've left cold.
You were the heart of it all. I promised I'd never leave,
but my promise is now stretched thin,
a strand of sugar pulled across continents.

The truth is, I never left you.
Every step away from home is a step toward you
because your sun still burns in my veins,
and I wear your warmth,
like gold,
like memory,
like I never left.

11. Old Lingering Hallways

The hallways hum with a dialect
I don't recognise anymore—
their tongues are loud, lacquered with laughter,
but not yours.
We sat like books pressed side by side,
spines aligned, stories bleeding into one another.
For three years,
like the punctuation in my sentence,
anchoring my wandering thoughts,

You never asked me to be more than I was.
When the others whispered behind glass walls,
you stood outside with me,
hands open like an embrace,
a quiet place where I could finally rest.

I think of how you balanced—
tightrope walker, diplomat, guardian—
never asking me to be someone I wasn't,
never making my solitude feel
like a punishment.

In the softness of her presence,
I found the strength to breathe,

a quiet pulse in the noise of the world,
like a flickering light that refuses to go out,
even when the shadows consume the edges.

Now, I drown in the soft current
of new friendships,
their kindness thin as paper.
when I chose silence over the clamour,
You nodded as if it were poetry.

I wish you could see me now,
how I sit in crowded rooms
and still feel
like a tree in winter,
branches bare, roots restless.
my steps echo like questions
no one will answer.

If I could send you this letter,
I'd fold it like a paper crane,
tuck it into the old hallways
where our whispers still linger.
the wings folded tight,
but with every gentle breath of wind,
it would unfold back into the spaces we once shared.

12. Lantern Shaped Like Laughter

I tell you, it's like carrying an ocean in my chest,
this ache of leaving, of untethering,
like the strings of my past cities have unraveled
into a mapless sea I cannot swim.

But then there's you—
a lantern shaped like laughter,
your voice a steady hum that carves the fog away.
You carry me the way a father carries
a child too stubborn to admit they're tired,
soft but stern, always knowing what I need
before I ask.

When I landed in India,
my suitcase and my skin heavy with distance,
you were the first face I found—
wide as sunrise, arms open as if to say,
"Here, put it all down."
And I did.

You wouldn't let me touch a dish
or lift a single shadow.
It was as if you were scrubbing the homesickness

off my bones,
washing me back into someone who could stand again.

You are the kind of friend
Who takes the weight of my world
and spin it into something light—
a kite, a joke, a moment
I can tuck behind my ear for later.

In your presence,
I am reminded that belonging
isn't just a place or a person—
it's the quiet ease of being seen,
the simple comfort of knowing
I'll never have to navigate alone.

13. Pixelated Applause

They say "dream big," and so I did—
not knowing that dreams have sharp edges
and no instructions for how to hold them.
Now I sit in rooms where my name is called,
spoken in accents that once twisted my own,
rooms where people clap
and the sound feels like rain falling in a place
that has forgotten storms.

I have achieved what I set out to:
stepped into a life I couldn't imagine,
climbed a ladder I couldn't see.
The emails and the nods of approval—
they come like coins tossed into a wishing well,
rippling in waters I can only watch
through the glow of a screen.
I stand there, grateful,
but unsure of what I am wishing for.

I hold my triumphs like fragile birds
in my cupped hands,
but when I open my palms,
there are only windows to faces,
their smiles pixelated and distant.

Joy becomes a muted echo,
dancing across cables and satellites,
returning to me as something thinner,
less alive.

I think of home, of voices that knew me
before I became this version of myself.
They are there, in tiny boxes,
cheering from living rooms I cannot step into.
I see my mother raise her hands in prayer,
my father nodding with pride,
their presence close and far all at once,
tied to me by a thread of wi-fi and longing.

Here, joy is lonely but shared.
It sits at the table with me,
folding itself into the silence between calls.
I eat my successes with a screen's blue glow,
the warmth of their applause reaching
but never touching my skin.

I wonder, is this what winning feels like?
A celebration held at arm's length,
a closeness that never closes?
I pile achievement on top of achievement,
but the view from the top
still looks pixelated, framed in glass.

What is joy when it comes in delay?
What is pride when it travels halfway across the world?
I sit with my success and try to hold it,
to see their smiles and make them enough.
And for a moment, it almost is—
a connection that slips through my fingers,
soft and sharp as the dreams I started with.

14. The Festival In Grey

In my home, Diwali is a sunburst:
oil lamps flickering like heartbeats on the threshold,
their flames licking the hem of the night,
turning darkness into something holy.
But here, it is just another day.
No gold smeared across the sky,
just the grey of routine pressing its thumb
against my chest.

Ganapati once lived in our front room,
his clay body heavy with prayers and hisbiscus.
We whispered our wishes into his ears,
watched his wide belly grow with blessings,
sent him back to the rivers to carry us forward.
But here, the river is a road,
and it swallows me whole.
I see him only in my memory—
a god of beginnings I left behind.

Navaratri was the sound of bells and anklets,
our voices braided in songs that wrapped
the house in musical devotion.
Nine nights where even the moon
danced in our honor.

But here, my nights are silent—
just the hum of a kettle,
the glow of a screen.
I turn my face to the window,
but the stars don't sing back.

I act like it's a normal day:
a lunch break spent scrolling through photos
of faces that look like mine,
smiling in the glow of a home I no longer stand in.
The ache is quiet but sharp,
like the edges of a diya before it's lit.

Here, in this city of strangers,
no garlands draped over gods,
only the muted hum of the world moving on.
I close my eyes and imagine the warmth
of my family's laughter,
their joy a festival I can't join.
I wonder if they feel the absence of me
as I feel the absence of them.

I tell myself this is temporary,
that next year I'll light the lamps,
I'll sing the songs,
I'll kneel before Ganapati and press my palms together.
But tonight, the emptiness hums.

I hold it gently,
like a sparrow in my cupped hands,
and hope it will fly back home.

15. A Home In Your Throat

There are words curled at the back of your tongue—
waiting, like hushed children behind curtains.
Vowels cradle themselves beneath your tongue.
Consonants click against your teeth, restless—
An alphabet of ghosts you summon in private.
Your throat holds rooms with locked doors.
The language of your mother, your grandmother,
Rests heavy, like their warm hands on your shoulders.
You do not speak it here,
in this borrowed land,
where your voice is a suitcase, always half-unpacked.
Sometimes, you swallow them whole—
Those words you long to share.
They dissolve, bitter and familiar,
like medicine choked down without water.
You walk through markets, coffee shops,
carrying two tongues:

One you dare display,
The other hidden—
like a letter folded tight,
words pressed flat, breathless in the crease.
But at night, in a quiet room,
You speak to yourself,

to family and friends back home,
fluent and unfettered.
Your words unfurl like midnight flowers,
carrying the scent of distant soil.
And one day—
Someone will hear the home in your throat,
see the welcome mat behind your teeth,
and answer back, in your language,
as if you both knew the way all along.

16. The Wound You Cannot Touch

You're a ghost dragging its own body,
each step another reminder—
too much flesh in a place made of paper.
Your hands don't fit in the spaces between strangers,
and your tongue stumbles over foreign syllables,
too thick to be understood,
too soft to be heard.

Every corner you turn,
you are lost—
not in the streets,
but in the hollow of your own chest,
where the ache of home is a wound you cannot touch.

You try to build yourself here,
a house of bricks and borrowed words,
but the walls are thin,
and the roof leaks memories
that you can't stop gathering,
stitching them into the fabric of your soul
like they'll keep you warm at night.

You are a suitcase that never quite closes,

always packing and unpacking,
the things you leave behind
and the things you've yet to find
too heavy to hold.
And when you look at the sky,
it is not yours—
it doesn't know your name
or the roads you used to walk barefoot on.

The nights here are endless,
the kind that swallow you whole,
and you wonder if this is what it means
to be both too much and never enough—
to live in a place
where you can never belong,
no matter how hard you try.

But still, you breathe,
even when the air tastes wrong,
even when you are drowning in your own silence,
because the memory of home
is a flame that refuses to go out,
burning in the deepest part of you
where nothing else can reach.

17. Ghosts In My Pocket

I came here with a bag full of promises
and a tongue tied in knots.
I walked these roads
like a girl with broken shoes,
fingers curled around the hope of fitting in—
but homesickness was a shadow I couldn't shake.

I kept talking to my ghosts.
The voices in my head had better directions
than the maps in my pocket.
I wasn't alone,
I had voices—
voices from back home,
but they were whispers through glass,
ghosts in my pocket.

Their laughter felt like paper,
thin, too far to touch.
They spoke my name like it was a foreign sound,
and I couldn't hear it properly.
I tried to feel them,
but their words fell like rain on dry earth,
and I was the soil that couldn't drink it.

I don't know why their presence didn't fill the empty,
but it didn't.
 I was standing in a crowd of ghosts,
and still, I was alone.
I cracked open my bones,
waiting for something to grow back,
but all I could taste was the salt of wanting.

My legs didn't know how to walk here,
I kept tripping over myself,
falling forward with no cushion,
the city's concrete floor too cold
to catch my weight.

Some days I thought I might drown in the noise,
the echo of my own mistakes
ringing louder than the trains.
But I'm still here,
rebuilding my skeleton,
shaking out the cracks like loose coins,
slowly finding balance in the mess of it all.

I'm learning to speak this language,
but my words still slip like oil,
never quite landing the way I want them to.
My voice is a wrecking ball,
crashing into walls I'm still too afraid to climb.

It doesn't feel like home,
but it doesn't have to.

I've learned to stand up on my own—
even if the ground beneath me
feels unfamiliar.

I am learning how to walk again.

I am learning how to walk again,
one fractured step at a time,
and though the bones ache,
I feel the strength in them now.

18. Litost in Translation

They look at you, puzzled,
and you feel the ache—
an exile who mistakes a prayer for a curse.

Every question they ask is a fogged window,
and you are there, tracing answers with your fingertip,
only for the heat to devour the meaning.

They say, "I don't understand,"
and suddenly, neither do you.
You become a city of closed doors.
Your own thoughts whisper behind locks,
and you're too afraid to turn the key.

You find yourself in new skin with new syntax—
slippery as fish, yet shimmering in the light.
The woman you are becoming stands at the water's edge,
calling back to the girl still drowning in the past.

Sometimes, you look in the mirror
and see an empty suit wearing your face like a borrowed
dress—
its seams stitched with doubt,
its fabric unraveling at the shoulders.

Imposter, you call her.
As if change were a crime,
as if growth were a betrayal of who you used to be.

But there's a language in the ache too—
like the bruised bloom of a dawn sky
just before the sun arrives.
A new flavour softens your mouth,
its taste unfamiliar, but sweet.

You learn that understanding is a slow wind,
that you are allowed to mistranslate yourself,
to be both a question and an answer—
hesitant, but whole.

One day, you will look at your reflection
and whisper, "Here I am," not with shame, but with a
quiet pride—
like a door creaking open,
like the first word spoken after years of silence.

A bridge, finally spanning the distance—
between your mouth and their ears,
between who you were and who you are becoming.

19. The Lighthouse

There is a crack in my skin where home used to be,
a splintered map folded wrong, edges torn,
and you,
In the absence of family,
you were hearth and hymn,
the body I leaned on when mine collapsed.

You, with your hands stained by my grief,
your spine curved under the weight of both our skies.
Who else could bear such quiet wreckage
and still bloom like violets in the snow?

The days unraveled like old tapestries,
Each thread a new kind of ache.
I remember the nights I unspooled myself,
A broken film reel of worry and silence,
and you stayed-
with every sigh, every storm, every fevered night,
you stayed.

Even in the moments you broke,
silent cracks hidden behind your smile—
you held the weight of us both,
like Atlas carrying my world and yours.

How cruel it is to love someone
and burden them with yourself.
How many nights did you stitch your own wounds
with trembling hands,
only to hold me together when the morning came?
And in this foreign land,
where nothing felt like mine—
you were.

When I think of you now,
it is not with guilt or sorrow,
but gratitude so deep it burns.
The year has passed, but its shadows linger,
etched into the lines of our hands,
the quiet corners of our hearts.

And though our journey has shifted,
its whirlwind calmed,
Not a goodbye, but a new beginning—
a promise that even in separate worlds,
you are woven into mine.
For you are not just the echo of my survival,
A friend, a sister, a lighthouse—
you are the shore I will always return to.

20. Suitcases Packed With My Soul

Memory is a suitcase,
always packed, always unpacked,
bursting with the things I left behind
and the things I gathered.
Each goodbye a zipper that won't close,
each hello a tear in the fabric.
The weight of the past in my hands,
never light, always unfinished.

I am an airport at dawn,
my family folding into me like creased clothes,
every goodbye a torn sleeve,
every hug a suitcase packed with words unsaid.
My aunts and uncles, faces smudged with time,
hold onto me like fragile promises.
Before my flight, they never let me go—
roots binding me in place,
their smiles warm in the folds of my coat.
I packed their love in my bag,
its weight too much to carry,
but I never leave it behind.

I went to my aunt's and uncle's,

and every time, she cooked my favorite dish,
though the whole house was tired of it,
her hands steady with the love she never measured.
Each meal tucked into my suitcase,
a small comfort to carry when I'm far away.

My uncle always served it,
His smile the only thing warmer than the food,
because he knew it was never just about the meal,
but the comfort of a plate served with a piece of home.
I pack his kindness in the corners of my heart,
folding it carefully so it won't fade.

The keeper of my grandmother's days,
eyes wet with goodbye,
tucks her heart in the corner of my bag,
like a letter I'll never read.
Her love lingers,
heavy and precious,
a memory that never fits quite right
but always finds space.

Caught up with an old friend
in the same café, with the same menu—
hot chocolate, cinnamon roll, iced coffee.
Each word we spoke falling like a soft landing,
the comfort of being seen,

of unpacking the weight of old suitcases
with someone who knows exactly what's inside,
wrapped around us like the aroma of cinnamon in the
air.

When my flight landed in the middle of the night,
my cousin met me with sleepy eyes and a quiet smile.
She had cooked a meal before I arrived,
heated the food, laid out the plates,
and made the bed while I washed the travel off my skin.
A warm bundle of companionship,
folded neatly into the corners of my suitcase,
to carry forward when the road gets lonely.

My teacher, confidant and mentor,
taught me to breathe in stories,
Without her, I wouldn't know how to carry their weight,
each line a lesson in how to wear a role,
how to own the stage of my own life.
like bags stuffed with everything I've forgotten
but cannot forget—I pack her lessons in the pages of my
mind.

Caught in books,
pages peeling from the spine,
my English teacher in middle school
letting me read through the cracks of lessons,

leading me to worlds I could hold in my palms.
I fold those worlds neatly,
like shirts that never wrinkle,
but always remind me of who I was.

The lake outside my window, an old friend,
it's surface still enough to remember the days
I sat waiting for her,
my best friend,
a clock ticking in the rhythm of our feet.
I pack the sound of her laughter,
the quiet of our shared time,
tucked into my suitcase like a photograph I'll never lose.

My mother knew without looking
when I was crying in the silence of my room,
sleeping beside me like the softest promise,
her body the quiet strength I leaned into.
I carry her warmth,
soft as the pillow she once shared with me,
tucked into the corners of my heart.

My father's voice is the weight of care,
paying for my peace when I couldn't bear to choose,
his love hidden in meals I didn't ask for but needed more
than I knew.
I pack his voice in the folds of my mind,

the echo dictating the OTP forever with me.

Grandmother, small and tired,
walks to greet me like a moon at earth's edge,
each step a prayer.
I am the air that remembers how to breathe her in.
Her footsteps a memory that weighs heavy,
a part of me that won't fit in the bag,
but I carry it anyway.

My sister, keeper of my chaos,
fills my water bottles with love,
a tether pulling me back when I am too far gone.
I pack her laughter,
her quiet strength,
the way she never lets me go.

I walked the highway after midnight,
with friends and lovers who left dust in my mouth
but no trace in my heart,
wondering if I was ever free or just carried away by the
wind.
I pack their shadows in my suitcase,
the ones who were never meant to stay,
but linger in the edges of my journey.

My best friend ran through the airport,

legs the rhythm of goodbye,
always faster than I could catch her.
And somehow, we always made it.
I pack her love in the space between heartbeats,
the way she always ran to me,
and I never had to ask.

The night we ran for a train in Delhi,
he didn't let me pay the porter,
our feet a thrum of life in a borrowed city.
I pack that night in the seams of my coat,
the feeling of running towards something
and never looking back.

I lived in libraries,
sifting through pages like I was searching for something
lost.
The world turning,
and I danced too much,
pretending I wasn't running from memories left behind.
I pack the scent of books,
the rush of deadlines,
the weight of every page
holding my past in their creases.

I learned to make new friends,
unlearning the ones who bruised my heart,

sitting with myself,
finding comfort in the silence,
a soft symphony playing just for me.
I pack their faces in the corners of my mind,
each one a stitch in the fabric of who I am.

Pushing a cart with 23x3 suitcases,
each one packed with memories too heavy to forget,
sending them off like dreams through the baggage claim,
the weight of my past tucked into every zipper and fold.
My memories sealed in the belly of the plane,
heavy with things left unsaid,
the weight of all I left behind
flying with me into the sky,
each suitcase a part of me,
a part of the story I carry on my shoulders.
Each suitcase, a reminder of who I was,
who I am,
and who I will become,
folded neatly into the corners of my heart.

21. The City That Learnt My Name

This city did not greet me with open arms.
Its streets twisted like an unfamiliar tongue,
its skyline a furrowed brow.
its skies stretched grey and wide,
its rain fell sharp and cold—
not a welcome, but a test.

I was the intruder at its table,
a voice out of place in its crowded rooms,
the echo of my own footsteps
drowned in the murmur of a language
that folded itself around me,
but would not let me in.

I arrived as a question,
a voice swallowed by the hum of trains,
the shuffle of feet on damp pavement.
It ignored me,
busy with its own rhythm,
its own endless, ancient stories.

I learned it in fragments,
the way you learn a stranger—

by noticing the small things first.
The way the light clings to brick
like it belongs to it,
how the Thames breathes in and out,
steady as an old clock,
how even the pigeons
move with a kind of certainty.
The soft glow of lights on brick,
how they flicker in the early dark
like the city is winking,
but not at you.

This place is not a lover,
is not a lover, but a teacher—
impatient, sharp-tongued,
but generous in its lessons.
It taught me how to sit in silence
on a train packed with strangers,
how to lose myself in its maze of streets
only to find the way home
was always a turn away.

I stumbled often,
but the city never stopped moving.
Now, it knows me too,
in small ways—
the cadence of my walk on its streets,

the way I wait at crossings
as if it's testing me,
and I am patient enough to pass.
It has learned my name
in whispers:
spoken by the wind,
tapped out in the rhythm of rain,
etched in the footprints I leave
on its worn-out stone.

This city and I are still learning each other.
It holds my name now
like a friend who hesitates
but gets it right.
I will never belong to it fully—
but in the quiet moments,
when the river breathes
and the light softens,
I know I belong in it.
And that is enough.